Paeans

In addition to about twenty other works, the following twenty-nine
poetry volumes were published by the author:

TAVASZ, 1948
FROM BUDAPEST TO TOKYO, 1957
SUMMER FLOWERS, 1960
AUTUMN DANCES, 1963
TS'AU MOU, Chinese tr., 1966
WINTER TUNES, 1974
POEMES CHOISIS, French tr., 1975
SPRINGTIDE, 1976
SELECCIONES DE DANZAS DE OTONO Y
    FLORES DE VERANO, Spanish tr., 1980
O:GALTI DIVALO, Gujarati tr., 1980
OFF SEASONS, 1981
COLLECTED POEMS, 1981
POEMS OF JESUS AND OTHER POEMS, 1982
HOLINESS IN A WORLDLY GARMENT, 1984
CHUI WU, Chinese tr., 2d ed., 1984
SPELLS, (Ut pictures poeta), 1984
EUROPEAN ODES, 1985; 2d ed., 1985
ODES EUROPEENNES, French-Engl. bilingual ed., 1986
BOOK OF DITHYRAMBS, 1986
ASIAN ELEGIES, 1987; 2d ed., 1987
SPACE ECLOGUES, 1988
COSMOGRAMS, 1988
NOVA COMOEDIA (Part One), 1988
ELEGIES ASIATIQUES, FRENCH TR., 1991
NOVA COMOEDIA, Part Two, 1992
NOVA COMOEDIA, Part Three, 1992
CELEBRATION OF LIFE, 1992
IDYLLS, 1992
EUROPÄISCHE ODEN, 1992

PAEANS

JENO PLATTHY

FIPA of UNESCO
SANTA CLAUS, IN 1993

Copyright © 1993 by Jeno Platthy
Library of Congress Catalog Card Number: 93-73828
ISBN 92-9042-033-2

Cover design: the author's crocheted concert piano cover (*First Idyll*).
Photo courtesy Matthew Wollenmann

Manufactured and printed in the United States of America
First edition. First printing.

CONTENTS

PAEANS

PART TWO

**A POETIC RECORD OF MY BEING
    THE GUARDIAN OF HER DREAMS**

PART THREE

**NOVA COMOEDIA, Pt. II, four new Cantos
    MODERN SATIRES
        F) GULLIVER AMONG THE WINGED HORSES III**

        G) THE EGGHEADS

        H) THE RUM AGE

        THE INNOCENTING PROCESS

PART FOUR

TELEPHATIC SONGS

PART ONE

I

The Amazons in Ephesus

In the mythical past, many thousands of years
ago, the Amazons embarked on a mission
from Plato's famed Atlantis, where all the gods were
born and from where religion spread all over the
world. Under Queen Myrina the Amazons saved
the Atlanteans from the Gorgons, this Plato failed
to mention. During their military campaign
they conquered the East as far as Arabia
and Syria and then marching onward throughout
10   Greater Phrygia, they stopped at the Aegean Sea.
A number of cities were founded by them there,
such as Kyme, Pitana, Priene and the
sun-adorned Mytilene on the island of
Lesbos, this last one was named after Myrina's
own sister who took part in the campaign.
In the embrace of the gentle hills Smyrna was
also founded by the Amazons as was the
foremost city of the region, Ephesus, near
the river Kayster. There a shrine was established
20   where by the crowd the cult statue of Artemis
Polymnastus was worshipped. This Artemision,
the temple of Artemis as was called later,
was one of the seven wonders of the ancient
world. Artemis, "the untouched one" in the local
language, was born there, on Mount Nightingale, which was
the site of the original old Ephesus.

The large double colonnaded Artemision
overlooking the river enlarged into a
lake. With the background, the courtyard of many white
30   colonnaded sentries, extending to the left
and right in considerable distance, the shrine
stood as a monument to imagination,
ingenuity, a devotion to a great
Anatolian goddess who was kind to the
folks. They say that she was "many breasted", but it
is not true, for the breasts on her chest did not have
nipples, - they were rather eggs or palm-dates hanging,
and symbolizing fertility on a scale

that is no longer known. On the top of her high
triple crown was the replica of the temple,
her own, as if to say: love me as you love love,
for above the winged griffins of time, love, too, flies
away, faster than lives.
                              The lions on the arms
of Artemis, the female oxen, the fillies,
the bitches and the nannies on her body, an
array of neatly arranged small sphinxes with the
indistinct zodiac around her neck, below
that archaic smile which made Greece so famous in
her sculpture later, - and the crescent moon on her
forehead, - represented life, that bustling, ever-
moving mirror of uninterruptible flux
that teems the earth. She also bore the symbol of
the bee, the emblem of Ephesus, from a time
when the city was studded with flowers and in
the rivers the heavy sunshine as honey flowed.

Blame should go where envy belongs, for the pride of
the city, those eminent men who lived there, will
live forever. Even if for a single man
we'd like to visit the city, if such a trip
would be possible, it would be Heracleitus,
whose thoughts dwarfed the universe and everything in
it.We can visualize him as he was walking slowly
with his book in hand toward the Artemision.
But he was not alone although he stands out far,
far over the dark year-thousands, as a genius
of godly proportion. Michelangelo said
in a sonnet, he would give everything for the
sorrows of the exiled Dante, likewise we could
have given many things to meet Heracleitus.
There were also poets, such as Kallinus and
Hipponax living here, who believed with others
that poetry is not possible if it does
not roar like the waves of the stormy, wine-red sea.

Choruses of nine-year old girls sang as they drank
in the world, without limit: miracles of the
sunsets, deep red like freshly pressed wine, butterflies
as huge as a house or a garden, attachments
that shine as light-forests over aeons of time.
Hearts became little bells and they were tinkling and
chiming as well as blooming with a sweet fragrance

that flew in the air with unforgettable words.
Even the eyes were singing hymns as they did dance
and the message of these songs seems to live forever...
The whirlwind of beauty often tosses a soul
into spheres from which it never can return to
the daily chores where the worries are endless like
the sea. We are looking for something in the sky
which can be found only inside the heart, within.

City, where night-lights were burning, surpassing Rome
90   in this civilized invention, first established
in Ephesus on the earth, this great city was
carrying on the tradition of the Magna
Mater, Artemis, the lover of all living
creatures, when, following the Apostle St. John
who died here, Mary came to spend the last of her
years on the slopes of the mountain overlooking
life below. We wonder how come that life, dreams and
love are locked tight in the body as the twilight
braids into the hair the perfume of night-blooming
100   star-flowers, joy, faith with the kiss-taste of the wine?

II

The Full Moon Over Izmir

Wine-taste of the kisses, as the Pramnian wine,
the beverage of heroes, we tasted in Izmir,
the ancient Smyrna, where Homer was born. Wine was
a kind of posset: the mix of cheese, honey, milk,
curdled with grape drink. The gentle breeze fueled the
passions from early spring till late autumn and the
thoughts that reached into future, even of those who
were prejudiced. For there are many who speak and
write and live in vain, whose environment is an
anti-world because they never converse with clouds
and know not devotions which'd lift them up from earth.

The palm lined promenade of the seashore becomes
synonymous now with glory as it creeps and
keeps coming back. Hearts burn as fire-nests and the
flames of eyes never let people desire sleeping:
Niobe weeps in her stone-encrusted state as
our unbridled boasts provoke envy in others.
The mound of Tantalus still reminds the fools:
our unpaid credit cards hang right above our heads
as rocks that may fall down on us at any time.
But a blessing silence covers the fields and the
winter-snakes, the smoke lines, are released from the roofs
when one measures from the sanctified solitude
of the mountain-slopes whether the blueness of
the bay matches the spotless azure of the sky
and whether life, that presents everything so dear,
might shine on us with the full moon over Izmir.

III

Sunset in Aphrodisias

City of Aphrodite, being close to eight
thousand years old, settled first in Babylonian
time, was a cult-center. When I viewed it from the
Stadium as the setting sun was gilding the
ruins, my heart turned into a well. I always thought
that if there will be an autumn in my life then
you should be there with me, if Aphrodite grants
us the honor. I know lovers kill each other
with kisses in this summer, and whatever one
wanted once inside was already bestowed: the
sun, a butterfly, danced behind my sweetheart,
flittering on the shallow water of the Odeon.
Nearby tourists were bragging with their old rebuffs,
overbearing women who could not cease to talk,
with fingers crossed, interwoven so tight as chain-
links in a fence and those who always sow only
but never harvest in life. For the unmarried
ones the promises are given but these will be
forgotten as soon as they tie themselves down.
If immortals could cry for mortals, I think
Aphrodite, Artemis would be weeping for
them now. The birch trees next to the Propylon were
measuring silver with their thumb-size leaves in the
breeze. As soap-bubbles imitating rainbows,
my bride's skin was lighted by a subtle torpor,
sparks from the pink marble seated Aphrodite,
that spread and radiated around like the heat.

IV

Side in the Sunshine

When the light-lint and light-silt from the sea shift to
the Agoras and the Nymphaeum outside the wall,
ruins come alive. An enchantment rules over the
months and years. Statues designed as flowers, faces
built of decorated leaves and petals. On these
statues the mouths bloom like lilacs in the springtime
and one can detect the dream-wings over delicate
shoulders. Very silent poems praise the times when
the theater with its magnificent three story
10   skene was full of entertainment, including
naval battles in the flooded orchestra. The
dash for luxury and wealth made the citizens
complacent: they didn't want to arrive anywhere
for they lived in the present which was limitless
and always new... The pitfall of societies, the
crushing urgency of time was far from them, for
time is a piece of glory, a shining moment
of an individual or of a nation
that needs to be treasured. Only poets notice
20   that Nike does not have arms. So she cannot give.
She is only present as she represents the
victory but never the booty or the loot.
But no one has time nowadays to listen to the
whisper of the linden trees and no one has an
ounce of interest in researching or even
accepting the benign suggestions of the stars.

V

Morning in Aspendos

When seeing is melted into a musical
viewing and the music is supplied by the nigh
silent popping of red poppies and the purple
rosebuds on the fence, from the permanent springs of
the hearts a message wafts over which like a fragrance
says: perhaps I was only born now. The theater,
the best that ever existed and survived
from antiquity, with a perfect acoustics
echoes this unique and strange sentiment as if
the high-spanning hearts could be made into violins
and these would be sobbing soft. Gold sun-drops, pieces
of heaven, provide the power for anyone
to turn a minute into eternity while
golden lizards run between the ruins. They hide
an ocean which is ruled over by silence and
beyond the noise of the grape harvest something more
subtle settles in the town. Silence is as great
as a mountain. Indeed the Mountains of Silence
signal that the passing away will never reach
the soul and complaints do not befit anyone.
Thinking about these I'm watching her delicate
silhouette in front of the stone-stairs' empty stage.

VI

Moments in Perge

The try with which one'd reach up to the sky, to find
a metaphor, to illustrate the most prestigious
founding of Perge among all cities of the
world, by such poets and prophets as Mopsos and
Kalchas, Minyas, Machaon, Riksos, Labos as
well as others, is annulled by history since
the abundant sculptures, the inscriptions both in
the Pamphylian and Greek language are more
colorful than any comparison could be.
10   No wonder that in addition to athletic,
music and poetry competitions were also
held here. This was reflected by the movement in
the Temple of Minerva in Rome, on the
Aventine Hill, around Livius Andronicus
which developed into a *collegium poetarum*
at the end of the third century B.C. In
the net of the eyes the sky is caught where the pale,
spongy moon blends with the milky clouds, obstructing
any notion that the universe is endless
20   in time as it is infinite... Shadows under
the flowers or around the ruins are indistinct
and the art by which the causes of happenings
and the reasons of actions are discovered is
washed away. As a fragile airboat, transparent
like the wind, the large bouquets of the evenings are
tied to the season with moonshine and shooting stars.

VII

Patara. The Story of Santa Claus

The handsome triple-arched monumental gateway
still stands virtually intact, facing the large
theater in the distance, slowly overrun
by the drifting sand and the trees. Apart from the
wall of the mausoleum, the granary and
the cistern, there is not much left of the once great
city to see. In place of the ancient harbor
there're sand dunes now. Still this Lycian port is well-known
for a citizen who conquered the fantasy
of children around the world, particularly
in the North. Santa Claus was born in Patara,
in this ancient village on the Southern shores of
Turkey. When he was still a young man his parents
died, leaving him a considerable sum of
money. The young Nicholas used his wealth to help
the poor and the needy, knowing well that there are
things beyond the course of this earthly life which one
cannot influence, change, only alleviate.
The burden of seeing clearly the development
and actions of others and not being allowed
to help forced this young man to do his good work
in secret, without expecting thanks, praise for it.

Near Nicholas' home in Patara was living
an impoverished old man with three daughters, who
had seen better times before. The girls were renowned
for their amazing beauty, however, they lived
in a rundown house where many a time there wasn't
enough food to eat. The fate of the father was
already settled and sealed but he still worried
about the ending of his life, because in those
times it was out of the question for a girl to
get married without a dowry, to pay for the
wedding. It was at this time that the young Nicholas
heard about the plight of the girls whose lives went from
bad to worse, and instinctaneously, as they say,
he resolved to help them. He knew that they were not
suffering from zeroitis, the illness of
those who physically were all right but needed to

have the pretense of a malady. When the tint,
40   the lilacish hue of the autumn evening seemed
to stop for an hour or so, he slipped to the hut
of the girls and threw a little sack of money
through the open window. The girl's father made an
inventory of the future in finding the
money and realized that it was enough for one
wedding only. In his think'sgiving mood the young
Nicholas thought the pithybility of
his own action as someone who in his frightmare
calls a chokelet soonbolism of the taste, like the
50   fondness for sweets for instance, and discovered that
he did not give enough. Again he waited till
the sun was going down and was setting the
pine trees red along the harbor, - at that time the
sea licked the round building and the temple on the
shore. Whoever enchanced to see him then, he looked
like one dressed in red, hence the color of his clothes
was considered purple costumously. Yet once
again he threw another little sack of gold
through the window into the ramshackled house. The girls,
60   who lived in the hut as in a hobbyhole and
were permanently exiled in dreams, although they
never spoke a pitch-in language when playing their
boyler-girler games, started to hope, plan ahead.
The more so because one of the girls who combed her
hair with a toothbrush, peeked through the keyhole just at
the very moment when the money was tossed in.

Nicholas thought the dreams were like books from which
we always learn something. So he dreamed that he was
stingy and for the third time he paid a visit
70   to the home of the girls. But at this time there were
no windows open because the father of the
girls wanted to keep his money safe for at least
two of the daughters. Nicholas thought of the girls as
angels who kept their wings in storage boxes for
a celebration at the end of time, did not
want his gifts to be considered measlery, climbed up
the roof of the house and dropped his sack of gold through
the chimney. He was unaware of the fact that
the girls washed their stockings that evening and hung them
80   up to dry in the fireplace. Cascading down
the gold fell into the stockings where it was found
next morning. The father who was a glutton for

punishment before, gave an elaborate and
sumptuous wedding for each of his daughters, who were
living from then on happily ever after.

Unaware of the custom that people began
to hang up their empty stockings at night to find
them filled with presents next morning, Nicholas
went about his business as before, helping the
90   needy. Once when the mountains of Antalya
nearby were colored magenta over the sea
of Marmaris, he went to Jerusalem as
he thought he should before he gets much older. On
his return he settled in the town close by, in
Myra, at that time an important center of
Christendom. There many extraordinary
events happened to him, such as when one morning
he entered the church where the congregation was
augmented by a delegation of officials,
100   assembled there to pick the successor to the
Bishop who had just died. At the sight of him they
hailed him as their new Bishop. Stunned by this honor,
the congregation explained that they were praying
all night for guidance when a revelation in
a loud voice told them to chose as their Bishop the
first man entering the church in the morning. He
was that man of godly intention and desire.

Santa Claus performed many miracles, once he
even saved Myra from famine. Yet his interests
110   remained with children and young people like the girls
once who were able to be married with his help.

VIII

The Wonder of Hierapolis

In ancient times there was also a library
here as in Side. But the reason that the town
became to be celebrated in the past was
the existence of the Northern Grand Bath, Southern
Big Bath, the Nymphaeum with Apollo's temple,
the theater with the high reliefs and the place where
the Apostle Philip lived and died. And it's for
the calcium deposits of the hot spring, the white
clusters of giant bathtubs appearing as a
10   vast petrified cascade, the city is famous.
This sublunar landscape might not be paralleled
anywhere else on earth. The milk lakes of fairy
tales look like these terraces in their wintery
attire during the endless summers: loggias
and snowed-in balloons hanging on to each other
while the sky is sparkling blue above them. This is
the world of the frozen sunshine where one sits and
walks on mirrors, waiting to be duplicated
by them with travertine trees and fern gazebos.
20   A wonder-world made out of the purest cotton.

Legend has it that once upon a time a poor
woodchopper lived with his sister near a lake which
was overshadowed by large rocks. The girl did not mind the
poverty but her perceived ugliness really
bothered her as she never had a lover though
she had reached the age of marriage. One morning she
ran away from home and in climbing the mountain
she heard the voice of death calling. So she gave up
her life to eternity believing that her
30   existence on earth was meaningless. The very
same morning a prince from the nearby city climbed
the same mountain and as looking down from the heights he
saw the girl lying still near the little lake. The
rays of the sun as wrought-gold shone on the body
of the girl. The prince ran down to her and took her
in his arms. He wasn't certain whether she was
alive or not, so he washed her beautiful face with

water from the lake. She was revived by the warm
water and since then over the past two-thousand
40   years the spa as health-center cures rheumatism,
high-blood pressure and many other illnesses.

IX

Laodiceia

The best inscriptions and the artistically
designed sculptures, the carved columns were taken to
serve as building materials to the nearby
peasant houses, so there is hardly anything
left from the ancient city. But it was here that
in Cicero's time a flourishing colony
of Jews was guaranteed the freedom of worship
by the authorities. But even then they were
not free from vicissitudes. For it was their wont
every year to collect a sum of gold, to be
sent to Jerusalem. However, in the year
62 B.C., the Roman governor
vetoed the payment, confiscated the money
for the public treasury. The long series of
deprivations, restrictions was not started then,
it only exemplified that the selfless help
cannot be directed as one wishes it be
done. In the frame of silence memories are kept
and cheated by hopes one takes occasionally
what is rightfully his, in secret, his belief.

X

Kalocsa

Eleven hundred years ago the royal house
of Árpád settled down around this place, giving
their names to towns and fields up and down the Danube.
It was from here that Abbot Astrik obtained the
crown for the first Hungarian king, Saint Stephen
in 1001 A.D. The city was burnt and
destroyed in the wars during the centuries but
as seat of a cardinal for a millenium
it regained its gold glory at the end of the
eighteenth century. The unique library, pride
of the entire country, is dated from there. The
statues of Saint Stephen, Liszt and others are well
eclipsed by the art of the "painting women", the
superb embroidery and other customs, such
as the folkish "pillow-dance". In them the spirit
of a nation blooms that seldom ever had a
respite from calamity and almost never
a decade of uninterrupted happiness
as if understanding would have been chased away.

XI

Dunapataj

Our age is between two important periods, cleaved
after the world wars with the turmoil at the end
of the century and a dangerously great
unknown that surely will follow. So my being
here signifies a few weeks in six decades. The
artesian well and the hotel are gone: there are
other changes though. From the hundred-fifty-six
Jews who lived here when I attended Mrs. Kiss'
private Jewish School because German was taught there
10   in 1926, not a single one is
left. Few years ago even the Synagogue was
dismantled and the walled-in Jewish cemetery
locked that one should not try to visit it.
Now only the old know where it is located.
No wonder then that the wide streets are heavy with
melancholy, as Budapest with faces gone
long time ago. Knighted by sufferings, fate was
here to keep silence. And like someone whose mother
was a birdsong and his father a rare honor
20   of silence, thoughts bother me which so far never
entered a single earthling's mind, as if hidden
bells would be tolling from below the lake nearby:
this turncoat universe is not our real home, but
it only mimics the land where we all belong.

The much too sweet bunches of the vineyard were picked
by the birds and the bees as we were gathering
the raspberries in the afternoon. From our door
we saw heaven's gate. Our hearts were pulsing on the
pear trees like an uppertunity, while the
30   light was full of sparkles covering up the big
world of Beyond. The uncertain, shifting rainbows
mirrored her smile as I was thinking what heaven
may offer me after I was presented with
her love since no one can hug me, ever, as she
does. The stars are shining only for her and me.

XII

Kecskemét

In the heaven of afterlife where knowing and
feeling, seeing and hearing, tasting and smelling
are one and the five wits are blended with them, the
music notes open and close flowers. They remind
us of the bell-ringing in front of the Town Hall
in Kecskemét, where the chimes and tones open the
hearts. But one shudders at the immeasurable
sufferings the city endured in centuries
past: souls must be blooming here to enjoy the sound
10   of music. The tones build a structure in the soul,
they create an experience which is unique
and which has outside consequences if one wants
to translate the effects to a moral language.
It will take three-four hundred years to get rid of
the residue of the pain and this is also
true for many other cities of the nation.
But then with the *Psalmus Hungaricus* of the
XVIth century Mihály Végh, the spirit will
bloom, heaventually the sounds will open up
20   an irrevocable empire of the soul.

XIII

Visiting Budapest After Thirty-five Years

Heroic cities like Budapest, withstanding fights,
many deprivations, misery and defeat:
where once even the poet discounting the nights,
went to bed early that he might not need to eat.

But in this world where the worry is always remade
there are no limits to the expanse of the thoughts,
Dante's hell is our home. And when a hand grenade,
Chernobyl, explodes, everyone has his own doubts.

What cannot be trusted to well-meaning, just words,
10   words that eyes cannot read, neither the ears to hear,
because the message is too powerful and it hurts:
only the hearts treasure it without any fear.

Very few people, almost none, can understand
what the dead talk about and what the angels sing,
but in the mirror of poems, the words demand
that fame should be lavished here above anything.

For words are the seeds of heaven, sown into souls,
away from hairraisers, harrassers and the jokes.
And the poet from faraway oceans and knolls
20   brings back near fifty-years' enchantment to the folks.

With miracle streets, silver domes, the feminine
city is a jewel on a long-lost bracelet.
Though even hopes were rationed once like medicine
by drops, healed by new joys, I'm amazeiated.

When one reads many poems, he believes the world
is a beautiful and uplifting place to live.
Beyond yes and no, in an awkward way the word
Budapest deserves is the ancient one: belief.

Blue and gold dizziness shakes the Danube below
30   the Castle Hill. The heavens' re lowered to the eyes
and in an end-of-a-summer sundown the glow
of billions of purple roses shines in the skies.

They were nailed there by boys of the Corvin Alley
and girls from the Parliament victorious in fight
and over their heroism as a monument the
blue silences are towering into the night.

XIV

All-Heart

There is a girl who has no limbs and no shadow.
Her arms are made of pink, small, decorative hearts,
woven, rather kneaded to each other like dough:
masterpieces ever created by the arts.

Her voice is murmur of mountain creeks, whispered
music, splashing on diamond pebbles, clean, august.
I dread the time when her words will be remembered
only from my poems as frozen from the past.

Her eyes are burning, purple hearts and I still feel
10   in my palms her face, endless fields of cyclamen.
Hero against himself, meteor of pure steel,
I heard her say to life's half silences: amen.

Now, when it's impossible to be good on earth,
one hides his poverty till death as a disease,
for his personality depends on the purse.
When autumn with the star-bubbles is on its knees,

she radiates like flame-foams of Aphrodite,
the sky's permanent Christmas tree from yore.
Presenting mountains as birthday gifts the mighty:
20   we'd live at many places but won't anymore.

The time will come, they say, which is already here,
when with the storms of gold our lives will be ensouled.
She is all-heart, anchored by flowers with a cheer.
If she says we are not alive, I'm consoled.

XV

Strolling on the Shore of Lake Balaton

The blonde lake wrapped itself into a brocade fog
which lifted long enough for us to see Tihany
with its Abbey across the opaque waves. There is
something eternal in the peace here. Since there are
no tourists around, it seems time is a human
invention, for it's the time of times we live in.
Eyes are misleading instruments and documents:
there are many things what we cannot see, only
experience and just as many things as we don't
wish to see. Occasionally segments of the
future can be shown to someone who's sweethearting
perhaps, being convinced that the abstract has about
as much reality as physical things. The eyes, like
our windows, are stuffed with heavenly dawns, colors
that are from beyond imagination, as are
our lives and hearts with goodies from beyond the earth.

XVI

Opera in Vienna

To Prof. Walter Stockert

In the roles of others we tend to see ourselves
and as Freud, who went to the opera but once
in his life and believed that every artist is
a neurotic but not every neurotic man
is an artist, we like to analyze what the
roles mean. To a feminist it might come as a
total surprise that one's mother was also a
woman and his wife with his sister are highly
respected as well as beloved ladies: heaven
shines through them. When we see Euripides'
Hippolytos or Richard Strauss' *Arabella*,
ethically we're not far from the ancient verdict
that love should not reach excessive proportions and
touch the marrow of the soul. For Hippolytos
veiled his head in order not to be polluted
by shameful proposals, - Arabella's father
tried to sell her and her sister. Strauss' magicstry
is well below Mozart's who a few times went
beyond the commissioned works and loveistic
phrases, earning him but lavish verbal profits.
We view the heroes as they are unsinging songs,
playing so lightly with truth that they try to buy
children from the gods since they dislike the female
sex, arguing that sensible men do not yearn
or like to be kings or presidents nowadays
unless they've really taken leave of their senses.

XVII

Recurring Thoughts

My poems are spiritual exercises,
I dreamt. My recurring thoughts took me from the dream
to the Danube which was calm and the outline
of the houses on the other shore uncertain
as mirrored. Then at home the shape of the room was
constantly changing, the furniture and windows
only approximately in their places as
if reality would have been busted or just
reorgynized. Like one who'll always be a clod
10   and looks at the river where something may turn up,
at the river where something is "Waterlooming",
meaning the destruction of ideas, achievements,
going away hopes,- we wait and use ourselves as baits.
But what can we catch by baiting ourselves? God? Can
the person who specialized in personal
injury cases advance to tackle grievances
of nations? To assess the totality of
sufferings? Is there, was ever there such a poet?
I dreamt poems are spiritual exercises, -
20   seeing it stated on the label of a jar
in which my poems were kept like medicine for pain.

XVIII

Theories of Dreams

It amuses me to see scientifically
proffered views about the reason and origin
of dreams as leftover memories, saved from the
previous day. Or current life problems, unresolved
emotional issues, worries. These pronouncements
about the chemistry and purpose of the dreams
are not too far from Freud's, who saw our mysterious
mental images as repressed wishes. Modern
researchers focus their attention on the brain
and try to find among the neuro-transmitters
the circuits where the visual processing from eyes
to waves occurs. How'sitis. How would people know
anything about the soul? How could one guess the
origin of the golden tables, the angel
ladies, the inner spaceships, the aural arms and
suddenly generated or computerized
spaces, the yearnings that live within since thousands
of years, almost forever, - the bird-like creatures,
and visions of forthcoming happenings, looking
down through a shaft of light on the galaxy where
the planets are revolving in an incredible
slow pace, - like in my sweetheart's dreams? The universe
belongs to us. Xenophanes asserted that
if oxen could express themselves they would state the
shape of their god is like an ox, the lions would
affirm that their god looks like a lion, while the
horses' drawing of their supreme being indeed
would resemble a horse. So are we with God. The
souls know God is invisible as they are and
like a vast energy field, disseminates love,
knowledge, light, and throughout the unspecified realms,
sustenance. For no heart-directomy can change
our being here, - not even the miremized listing
of glue-grass music, - our pain or gafficky mood,
the Pythian grief. Not even those who under
the guise of expertise or devotion offer
their own tergiversation of the dreams.

XIX

Konya. The Tomb of Rûmî

The autumn days are the hardest that contrast the
handcrafted brilliance of the trees and the royal
art of silence with the fast, noisy pace of life.
It is easy to believe that God has given
up on the world when one views the unending
crime-waves of the West, the blatant display of the low
sinstinct. On the other hand, visiting the green
tiled mosque where the tomb of Mevlana is draped
with golden threaded arabesques of quotes behind the
10   silver encrusted gate, the conical turban
symbolizes Rûmî's authority as once
he was rising above both worlds in a dancing
frenzy, tearing his heart to pieces and giving
up his soul. The Mevlevis still dance in our days
with half shut eyes as one of their white sleeved arms points
to heaven and the other one down to earth in
conducting and dispersing a power which they
receive in whirling. And there is a soothing rhythm
in the dance to the music of ney, rebap and
20   kudum, corresponding to the unending rhythm
of the planet's rotation which is in tune with
the returning and changing cycle of seasons.

Stepping up into the air after taking a
deep breath, one stays there, stands on nothing, - and then moves
that someone may walk under him,- floating left and
right, without ever positioning his body,
without moving an inch. And in this singular
sensation, in the constant returning to the
original starting point, looking so much
30   beyond life, one cannot be enchanted by what
he sees, and neither can he be attached to it.

The force of space is crushing. Experiences,
observations are scaled down to non-zero fields.
The overpowering energy of emptiness,
the hypothetical field of void into which
a matter-like substance is injected against
determinatious unmassed particles, equals

the changes made by the density of time. The
uninterrupted zero-energy motions
40   so sincerely danced out by the dervishes' art,
describe the transitions in which the symmetry
of forces changes not only the outlook on,
but also the structure of, the universe. In
this enphysics an unforce blends existence and
non-existence much above reality and
the cosmos is degenerated into a
nullifiable state. The energy walls, the
walls of unevents, the unwinding spaces snap
into nonexistence. Like a phlox, the flower,
50   the evening bows above the lives to protect them,
an accent circumphlox. The inwarding radial,
the topological constant of inwardness-
motions clasp infinity to our being like
a whip. To tie time to existence, to being,
cosmos, is too bold a thrust, dangerous and false.

The imperturbable motion of the soul, past
unshining lights, beyond the light-waves turns to
indirectional sources, inproperties where
the strain on time is absent as time is absent
60   with the big-bangery of grapefruit universe.
We express thanks with our eyes and ears and with the
beat of the hearts in the constant turning changes.
In the induced supergalactic abode the
invisualizable and illocalized
immotional crests present the notion that one
who mastered the whirling dance may turn now, propelled
by insolar streams, ingravity transducers,
may indeed practice and write poetry of praise.

The transitional plane of the soul expands
70   the strengthless and phaseless fields of forces as one
moves away from them, - from life as it blends with the
soulline eternative exertions. But one is
not looking for objects in the timelessness, for
unforming models of inaction, superlight
spheres and impulsars in coalescent states, because
space breaks down into hyperstructures that do not
extend to observational directions. There
are inangular functions and future blasts that
erode the perspectives, whiteshifted and sparing
80   experiences where the overall-less nature

of immateriality rises above the
superluminal spheres of the great soul-turbines.
Indominating we wonder at hearts that could
dance on a threadbare existence, a doubleness
which might unveil not only the structure of thoughts
but the fabric of these, tieing them with the most
subtle texture of ideas, dreams and the soul.
An apparition of oneself, like a mirror,
stepping beyond the picture reflected, image
90 that lives forever as paintings and photos do,
in such an inconspicuous manner as the
wind dances in Konya and the fountain waves roll...

XX

Not Since the Slow Demise of the Roman World...

Not since the slow demise of the Roman world, its
successor state, the Holy Roman Empire,
the Napoleonic wars, or the break-up of
the Austro-Hungarian Empire in our
century, can one witness such a tumultuous
event as the dissolution of the greatest
threat to peace, the monolithic Soviet system.
The Communists, keeping one-forth of the world in
slavery, outdid the most brutal forces of
10   history, massacring more of their innocent
peasants than Nero did the Christians or Hitler
the Jews. Because of the crimes, both took their own lives.
It is exciting to observe the collapse of
empires, if one stays above the happenings,
above the fray, untouched by the enormity
of afflicted sufferings. But who are forced to
see the slaughters and think of the madness released,
the years crush those with their abject degradation.

The West won. Another such Pyrrhic victory
20   would certainly sweep away the laurel crown of the
winners. The time of the guitar and the single rhyme
is gone, - no one proclaims glory for the age which
leaves the acknowledgement of its geniuses
to posterity. Contrary to a well-known
Mycenaean painting which depicts the march of
ass-headed men, - who were not monsters but the masked
participants of an age-old ritual, - our
contemporaries are unmasked monsters, who well
pretend deafness and escape from themselves, from the
30   responsibilities and thoughts to the outside
world. The masses laugh at things they should cry at, while
the poet, the modern hero of standing firm,
is horrified at those who are so heartless, the
quarterhearted ones, and sits benumbed in this Folly
Age. Paeanstaking though, in the larkest way he sings, -
remembering that once Ennius had three hearts, -
would it have been in Paeanderthal days, in the
dead of winter somewhere where the snow is piled high...

37

XXI

Paros

The coast rises from the sea with crags of reddish
marble as the horizon unfolds between the
fleecy clouds and the foamy waves. This is a small
island with a single mountain, as if to say
only one man was destined to be born here to
attain fame, however dubious. The monument
Archilocheion, where many of the poems
of the poet were preserved, was a unique
distinction, till date accorded to no one else.
10   The Spartans banned his books for indecency.
Good poems are separated from clowning lives, the
vindictive intuition and maladorous vice,
otherwise Swinburne's shrill and wearisome jingles
would never indicate talent, as the sorry,
incoherent splutterings of Pound cannot. The
unutterably dull, which's the judgment over
many poetic tries, extends to the circles
where the authors lived. Hesheorus, Themorus
or others who call themselves Damocrats or
20   Rap-publican'ts from cud, eating scrambled egos
for breakfast or just brain-flakes, for their appetite is
vociferous. These statuscope-seekers might better
be called Don'theyrians, since don't they put on the
eyelashes for horns, and don't they whimpishcate in
rustling poems on their littlest or grossest binges?

Envy is an incurable disease and so
is the uncontrollable temper, jealousy
or rage. At the end of life one may be sorry
to have been always correct in seeing and in
30   describing others as they were. Truth never will
make anyone free, in spite of the repeated
prattling of preachers, just the contrary, truth will
take a person prisoner all his life... And the
heroic kindness, which was not Archilochus',
Swinburne's or Pound's habit, forces us to detract
from their oeuvres, taking away what was intended
for time... As the wintery, leafless fig trees in

Paros resemble giant thistles with thorns to
stab, the flock of Canada geese in front of my
40   window, like a half-sunk flotilla, looking for
algae, all raise up their afts from the shallow lake.

XXII

The Bosphorus

Fifteen steps from eternity and a mile away
from the pressing problems of the world one felt, till
a surfaced submarine with its deadly load
passed by under the balcony of the hotel .
Once the dark blue Clashing Rocks, the Symplegades,
were here, but these went under water now with their
fearful iron mantles, under the blue-plowed sea
where the constant clashings can no longer be seen.
Dismissing themselves from life: the poet thought of
10   the seventy foot high fir tree in the garden
of the house where once as a child he lived, and his
wife thought of swimming in the sun as she looked at
the small mosques and Christian churches in the mirror
of the sea. Such a latter one 'bathilica'
she called. The light was splashing around like sword-blades
as if the giant bridge tieing Europe to Asia
would have been trying to accomodate, even
embrace, the hurrying. While fate was fattening
fears for a roast, the poet and his poetess
20   wife were manufacturing time: little lapses
that leap into immortality on occasion.
He said the second rule of thumb for poets is
the blissy ignorance of obstacles, being
snow-souled in an incessantness where to teach the
rivers to murmur and the sea to roar is a
fitting task. For lives are dandelion puffs, blown
by the wind, events, we so quickly vanish from
the earth, leaving behind only a sunset, like
the one they once observed over the Bosphorus,
30   engulfing both shores and the bridge in a lilac haze.

XXIII

Where are the Jewish Communities...

Where are the Jewish communities of Nippur
of the once mighty Assyrian Empire, -
what happened to them and how were they dispersed, - the
questions are still lingering on after many
thousand years. The historians say that at
the time of the Babylonian exile,
millions perished by the sword, by famine and by
pestilence or were carried away to distant
lands and were lost. After forty-nine long years of
10   exile the survivors returned, and rebuilding
of the temple commenced. The destruction of this
in A.D.69/70, sent tens of
thousands to the far corners of the world, fleeing
the ceaseless brutalities, massacres, pogroms.

Where are the Jewish communities of Nippur,
where are the Jews of Baghdad, Aleppo, Teheran, -
one asks, and as the diaspora embraces the
known world, we can also ask, where are the well-known
great Jewish enclaves of the ancient world today?
20   The first of these, known in A.D. 65, was
in China, after a massacre of Jews a
generation earlier cost the lives of at
least 50,000. Historical research
gives 1163 of our era when
a synagogue was erected in K'ai-fêng-Fu,
Honan province, under Rabbi Lie-wei, that is
Levi, following the exodus of A.D.
34. Many other colonies were then
established in Ningpo, Hangchow and elsewhere. But
30   where are the Jewish colonies of China now?

Where are the Jews who went to India down the
Malabar coast, the Bene-Israel south of
Bombay, the synagogues of Chennamangalam
and Mâla? Where are the dozens of other large
places of worship for the sons of Judah in

Asia? Or Dura Europos for that matter?
The authenticated chronicle of Japan,
compiled on the order of the Imperial
Court, states that during the reign of the fifteenth great
Emperor, called Ojin Tenno, a large group of
aliens, numbering near a hundred-thousand,
entered Japan in A.D. 216.
They were settled in Yamashiro, outside of
Kyoto, and called themselves Hata. Were they the
Lost Tribe of Israel? Hata-no Kawa Katsu,
building the famous temple Horyuji
of Nara at Uzumasa, erected within
its compound a small shrine, named Osaka Jinja.
The characters denoting Osaka in the
Japanese language are identical with the
signs of King David in the *Bible*, pronounced as
"Dapi" by the Chinese ever since. And on the
shores of the much sung Lake Biwa there is a shrine
called Aburahi Jinja, that's Abraham's Shrine.
Some even maintain that the Gion Matsuri
Festival on July 17th in Kyoto,
the Summer Festival, is derived from Zion...

The word-leaves from the tree of life stir up the pure
sentiments and heal nations plagued with problems. As
the star of David, the symbol is carved on the
stone lanterns along the sacred road of Ise
Grand Shrine, lit at night, history blends visible
with the invisible when darkness descends.

The inquery is painful, for the questioners
are penancing themselves in futile attempts
of listing the bloodbaths and trying to trace the
florid Jewish princedom of feudal France between
768 and 900 of our time.

God answers to none. Moses singed his lips in front
of the burning bush and so descended from the
mountain. Attuning myself to a different
wavelength, I am singing new songs as no one before.
I know that nothing is far today, nothing is
unreachable. I pray and hope the sufferings
of the year-thousands might end in a bonus and
we will learn and practice the art of being kind.

We cannot prevent anyone to ask questions,
just contrary, inqueries should be encouraged,
and alongside the uttered ones it also
80   should be asked: when will barbarism be ended and
when will we learn to behave as human beings?
How dare we open the doors of the past? Is the
past a crutch or a wing? Seeing our present troubles,
the misunderstandings, hatred and the crime, a
sigh-relief goes up from the cemeteries, the
dead are relieved that they are not living with us.
For no one can make the past unhappenable.

The too gruesome memories of the holocaust
and the accompanying spiritual horrors,
90   as the pain petrifies to a long wailing wall,
do prompt the souls in heaven to protest against
being born into our present circumstances,
which was purposely left out from my account of
the World Beyond Ours. For the first coherent words
of a newborn to the parents are: "Why did you
bring me into this hideous world? Why did you?"

Seeing so much ahead of time where time cannot
be seen, into a secret universe, an
alternate world, where the roots of sacredness reach,
100 one'd like to see the end of animosities,
enmities, see a celebration of events
centuries ahead, that have not yet been given a
name. And in that festive distance, untrapped by wealth,
unburied by memories of compassion,
tolerance and impearled kindness, the poet would
dream out loud, - freed from an intolerable weight, -
that all the past sufferings certainly were not
useless. When the sun hides in the thick bushes the
painorama is pressed into pure peals, tolls, as
110 the unward move of the waves knells, like the wisdom
of winters woven so wondrously with springs.

XXIV

Ars Poetica II

When the random orientation of fate and
the inward turn, the uninstinctual pulls
like dragnets steer someone toward poetry, the
person ought to be equipped with the stamina
and perseverance of an Olympic champion,
with the skills of a float-designer for the once
a year held Tournament of Roses Parade in
Pasadena, California, and with the
expertise as well as determination of
10   a scientist. The poet in question should have
as pleasing an inside as the winner of a
beauty pageant outside. Being familiar
with invisible lights, the fatalometric
unshaped, inwarped and discontinuous spaces,
the poet must think of the cosmos as a huge
uni-verse where immateriality is
the dominating force. Once Carol L. Abell
stated, the first rule of thumb for poets is a
solemn oath of poverty; the second says:
20   ignore the difficulties, as I said before.
The third rule of the thumb emphasizes that one
should beware of the addiction to vanity.
The fourth one prescribes the wearing of a hair-shirt
over the heart as not to be swayed by feelings.
Letters to God are directed to the Dead
Letters' Office, the poet is the anti-hero
from Heorshema after a bomb has been dropped.
The hieratic dignity of poets
is maintained by the immutability of
30   existence, by the ingravity forces and
the unpredictability theory of life.

When the highest expression was granted to man,
with poetry the nobility of love was
advanced. Poets are the wizards of grammar and
prosody as they must know more than enough of
the rules and inadequateness of the language.

Continuing my *Eleventh Space Eclogue*, the
poets still do not know the power they possess
and how to use it. Monumentality ends
40   where psychology begins: without restrictions
life is a raw material to work with. Fate
and soul are not separate concepts and those who
escape to the outside world from themselves cannot
embrace the world. Courting the angels when the loud
crickets're knitting their net in the evenings' silence
and the blue butterflies of the dawn are cruising
the darkness toward the coming day, poets build
a castle from tears and pave a rising endless
road with bleeding rose-red hearts, aligned by pure, white
50   calla-lilies to the skies. In the artistic
creations such an unheard-of richness and such
marvellous imaginations are portrayed which
can be found only at the bottom of the soul.

The language is changing. The "precipitation
system" was called rain when I was young, now
we've about "two inches of accumulation",
not being told of what, perhaps of "everything",
including excrement. Yes, when I was young the
childhood "attention deficiency syndrome"
60   and "motivation deprivation" were simple
laziness. Contrary to the motto of the
Olympic Games, the poet's slogan should require
him to go "slower, deeper and against the time."
In symmetry with infinity and with light-
walls of an unnamed empire which extends well
beyond the expanse of incoalescent forces,
the poet sinks into seeing and unseeing,
sensing as Darnecius once that there is a slab
on the Ouchitary Mountains with the saying
70   inscribed for the moremorans and the eitherites
who live around there, transcribed almost verbathim
in soughtful eyeorization from squawked gabbings that
can be read from miles: There is no more late than now.

I said the language is changing. In a Tongue-Dance
one humorously may list declensions with the
I-ness, U-ness, It-ness pronouns, the plural
Our-ness, Your-ness, They-ness or They-nesses occur.
Likewise other combinations of words could be
handled, such as Our-ward, I-hood, I-self, I-sore,

80   My-sore, Me-thography, Mice-self, U-sury and
so forth, like in a multiplocation system.
Twice-ness of me: mes; Twice-ness of you: yous; and the
Double-ness of you: W. Ex-samples can be
provided like un-bride-led, en-brittle-d, ab-bridge-d,
in-a-brie-ty, how-ever-ness and so on.
A second declension would run I-oh-no-sphere
against Here-less-ness or Her-less-ness, Ten-tickle-d,
etc., least at last one is lost in the
lust, for whoever speaks well cannot possibly
90   do thinking. *Lego ergo sum*, as once Mary
Juana and Mrs. Sippi stated, who were
not, nevertheless-bians, but considered the
tummy-hawk, absconditure and supersilence
as parts of the backlog on sorrows, as well as
hysterical imperatives, and not in the
realm of legislative poetry. But the
dualis: beinging as bingo: being-go,
dramma donna; or trialis: barbar bar, are
the main points of the new grammar. Exceptions
100   are: disguessing, liebility and other forms.

It is always a daring to express oneself,
to display the child by exuberance and by
enchantedness with the uniqueness of the world.
And to step into the line of great poets without
trepidation is almost foolish. But we have
to try. We must see as the trees are marching in
the brisky wind over the slopes of mountains, to
another range, another slope. Poets must see
the lakes' journeying along the trees, the endless
110   flow of rivers into another realm. They
must see the almost invisible motions,
that feelings come alive and must pay attention
to hunches to such a degree that they could sense
happenings in the coming years, indications
of changes, whatever is in store for mankind.
The poets must see the invisible signs. There
is a borderline between coming and going
into invisibleness: many times a poet
ought to travel that road with the great poets of
120   the past. For invisibility is not the
hell, although it is an unaccosted place, but
it is also the region of heaven from where
ideas, hopes, beauties and blessings are transplanted.

Oh, if the poets would see with me the person
into whose hands the stars slowly descended from
the sky last night as she was gently balancing them...

XXV

Ankara

The symbol of Ankara is the sundisk or
sistrum, an animal or stag figure in the
circle of the zodiac, a common feature
of archaeological excavations found all
over the Anatolian plateau. Some of
the statues in the museums, such as the baked
clay Mother Goddess or the gazelle shaped vessel
go back to more than eight thousand years, depicting
life as it goes on uninterrupted. The name
10 Anatolia means the land of the rising
sun, where art and religion, agriculture and
animal husbandry, the textile industry
and leather work were first known. Before the Hittites,
from the Old Stone Age on through the Chattis, people
lived here. The Urartians were followed by the
Phrygians and these in turn by the Lydians, the
Lycians and the Ionians of the Eastern Greeks,
but the highlands always were inhabited by
the local folk, unchanged over the millenia.
20 From Lake Van where the reflected mountains are twice
as high in the water, to the billowing Sea
of Marmara, the liquid gold sunshine pours and molds
over the hearts as it does the autumn landscape.
And little girls playing still prove that whose hair
is yellower than a pear or an apricot
should not wear a bow or ribbons, just fresh flowers
in it, tucked over the top or bent on the side.

XXVI

Space Age

Refraction makes the moon to be seen before it
appears: a new world emerges in the robe of
white azaleas and primrose, with much fanfare
and less serenity as it should. Hyper-light
velocities throw the images of sublime
prominences, aurora borealises
that are knotted and the occulted albedos
beyond the unsayable. The space age is here.

Assembly of mountain ranges and the stockpile
of springs, as there would be a storage for autumn
evenings, dusks and windless Sunday noons to replace
our lining up for hope, the revised and enlarged
hell of Dante. We're so glad to turn back on crime.

In my time man has landed on the moon, conquered
many diseases and introduced a legion
of electric gadgets. In my time Rilke, Yeats,
Valéry and Sandburg were composing their songs.
But in my time we have also reached the deepest
subhuman strata of mankind with Stalin and
Mao, - squinting at the garbage-headed flooziness.

As if slapping with a kiss, in my time many
worship star-like prostitutes. Decency and the
mentioning of morals provoke a guffaw and
patriotism means stealing state-secrets, for the
decay of social fabric and honesty is
the order of the days. Tapestry woven in
many colors: who wants to see the sunlight on
groundhog day? Words flow from the wound of the spirit:
a new intellectual world is being born and
while a numbness is hidden in everything, the
above brilliance, light-nature of the universe
eclipses the winters that ebb upon the hearts.

XXVII

The John F. Kennedy Center for the Performing Arts
in Washington, D.C.

The willows began to yellow and the sun was
setting over Arlington across the Potomac,
throwing its last golden rays on the red carpet
of the Kennedy Center for the Performing
Arts, to counterbalance the horrid spiritual
poverty which characterizes our age. On
the West side of the building the inscription quotes
"I look forward to an America which will
reward achievement in the arts as we reward
10   achievement in business." The words given by an
assassinated president might have meant for
a generation four-five hundred years from hence,
but certainly not for those who are carrying
on their professions in spite of the government.
A monumental meanness permeates this town:
the men are impolite, bribeable and unlearned.
The ability to argue doesn't have moral
standards: greatness is never taught today and the
wasted ingenuity betrays the trust of
20   the little people who still look toward this place,
the seat of government, for guidance, honesty,
compassion, care. Benefitting from the silence
of forthcoming decades, I have to state that to
the tasks one has to grow up, - which this city has
not done. The arms of the autumn around did not
cover the souls with gold: morally we are not
leading the world, we are misleading it. For it
is worthwhile to build a new, beautiful world if
man feels at home in it, his heart's attached to it.
30   The direction "up" often means to travel down
from a position in proper humility,
for greatness must stand the tests, verdict of the times.
Nowadays, when it is a crime to be a hero,
good men should be jailed in order to protect them,
because they are so few, so rare, they're so extinct...

XXVIII

The Degree of Reality

When the degree of reality is so great,
so overwhelming that it wipes out the sufferings,
joys, memories of all the earthly years as one
leaves this life, this cancelling out amounts to a
denial. Are we living off center? Are we
living misdirected, away from the goals which,
therefore, we'll never reach? Well, the super-Joycean
nature of the language, or handling of it, will
not reveal the fingerprints of infinity
10   on a leaf or thought, - even less the one who was
behind the act. All we're doing is borrowing
trouble instead of exercising the power
to still the motions, to stop the time for a while,
almost with a revengelical enthusiasm.

Beyond our lives lies the highest realm. The sets,
coordinates and the nature of that cosmos
are so much above comprehension that even
hints and parallel metaphors are pale, vain and
useless to approximate its reality.
20   Human concepts dwarf it. The manifestations
of its energies, dipped into love-enveloped
knowledge, tap the souls' senses, affirming that the
inner eye is indeed the sun and that in the
garden of existence human beings are heavens.

XXIX

Istanbul

Istanbul, - the name sounds as a faraway place
with romantic overtones, although nothing is
more far today than romantic feelings. Life is
lived to the fullest there even by those who are
tested by poverty as was Othello once. The
canned pain of food forces many to eat their own
words as perhaps Sisyphus did in antiquity.
He would be today only a fussy sissy,
unhuggable, useless, as a noberry pie.
We all repeat the childhood rhyme that sticks and stones
may break our bones but words can never hurt us, but
the truth is that words cut sharper than knives. Except,
perhaps, in Istanbul, in spite of the strangling
traffic and the tumult in the big bazaar, where
the bustling pace of life does not let us linger
on the past and the sorrows, where a song sweetly
sung reminds us that the world is at our doorstep...

XXX

The Airport in Bruxelles

We are attached to the world however much we
dislike it or despise it as we despise death
and look at it with contempt. Wherever we go
the battlefields are full of crosses, portraying
that killing is a pastime. Lives underlined by
permanent nights inside never reveal that the
self is a door only, to step through into a
higher realm. Leconte de Lisle, Hölderlin and
other good poets who broke through their most bitter
presents may have wondered: have we been the seas? At
the airport in Bruxelles, between two planes as well
as between continents, one laughs at the oneness
of life, the oncerity of our fate here as
I used to term it. While the sunshine filters through
the glass-plates and the big birds of planes come and go,
I think of the migrating souls between the tight
existences and a poetess' assessment
of my life-struggle as an uninterrupted
death-dance which is stretched for more than seventy years.

XXXI

Sequentia

It is your warmth which makes us not to feel the cold
at midwinter time when the snow is very high,
while the skeleton trees are covered with white gold
we know our special limb for pain touches the sky.

It is some light that emanates from you, wiping
away the fears before our entering the grave,
where the darkness then would no longer be rising:
in front of light-eddies a shore stands as a wave.

You are the knowledge a scientist stores in mind
10   and in the eyes of girls you are the shimmering.
You are the dream we leave with the morning behind,
a blessed encounter with the world, with everything.

And you never make us to be hesitating
although your nearness is an unbearable force.
Your handshake is totally debilitating
by pulling us into madness without remorse.

You draw our eyes away from the earth, into space,
where you then tie the thoughts with time into a knot
and bless all those who are believers and embrace
20   the real happy ones, for they're few and hard to spot.

We are religious but not in the strictest faith,
for faith is only a sign from you, it's a gift,
which is shown in a distress or in a disgrace
where we see with the closed eyes though we all are miffed.

Only you know whether there is still any stop
and how much is enough till the time will be donned.
An exact knowledge, - which we feel lives overlap,-
pulses in our arteries about the Beyond.

XXXII

The Words of a Bell

The seventy-two thousand angels and legions
of heavenly powers with drawn swords are only
opportunities, choices we may daily make
or miss. For there's absolutely no distinction
between the conspiracy of goodness and the
curse of grace. How significant it was for the
ancient Greeks that the Altar of the Dreams was next
to the Muses' Altar. For seeing and knowledge
are tied in the Afterworld. The words of a bell,
10   the undisturbed peace of the mine-fields of thunders,
the warning of a leaf-dance, try to say that we
carry experiences and memories over
but these have little value in the light of the
continuous change. Shackled in honey we learn
the highway to heaven is a toll road where one
needs to drop his intentions. Hate cannot be healed.
The plethora of light-beings, those who are in
spiritual forms and see future with the
irons in the fire, in a big fondue-pot,-
20   I keep my dreams in the sun. My best poetry
lines are those which I did not write down, - like the fire
in the summer roses that burns flameless all night.

XXXIII

In Contrast

In contrast to life in ancient times our small world
became colorless in the inside. True, we live
faster today than before, in a hectic way.
We observe, notice, more happenings than before,
but we fair poorly by comparison with the
citizens of ancient Greece or Rome. That above
the sky is not populated by gods and by
mythical beings, that our imagination
does not suppose rescuing miracles from heaven,
that the universe is not supernatural,
not tied to dreams but to chance collisions of some
electric and gravity waves, explosions of
supernovae, - that not only an Elysium
is not waiting for us but even Hades is
missing: this steals a piece away from the heart. To
see more clearly the eyes needn't be opened more,
but our perception does, the inner eye with the wide,
limitless horizon of thoughts. Perhaps we should
change the technique of understanding. It seems we're
only transient beings on the earth while life flows
between the soft hands. We try to regain that life
within which in antiquity was so open,
and elegant. We try to live in sanctified
solitude where we may view uninterrupted
the sustaining vision of immobility.
But is there hope that over the corruption and
crime the dizziness of eternal things would be
projected before the weak eyes with rare gifts from
the lap of ceaselessness to wipe away the tears?

XXXIV

Starting Point to Nowhere

Well, a city name might be substituted for
another one or used as a starting point
to nowhere because many people live a long
life without traveling anywhere. In old times
it was more frequent to stay put than nowadays,
though adventurous men are common to all ages.
When one lifts the veil of a name from a person,
city or a country, the ties will be clearer
and more intime. We do not go beyond knowledge
10 but with the method we go more far than wisdom.
Viewing the miracles of haystacks, raked and
stashed exclusively from bank-notes, money: the grades
of our inner life are directly connected
with eternity where the indescribable
greatness of humility is a force. Knowledge
leads nowhere. Expertise in a certain field, the
technical know-how of letting things work amounts
to the charming play of little girls as they pat
their cheeks with brushes to become red, alive...
20 Perhaps we should take the world once again into
the heart or rather the heart out into the world...

XXXV

Summa esoterica

The paincakes that are offered on visiting a
home, in seeing into the unbelievable
sufferings of men, the continuous daily struggle
that has no end, the worries, - one thinks that many
are presented with the crown of eternal life
and they have no knowledge of it. The hardest is
to learn not to wish anything from others, and
to offer understanding. Above the crude and
unbending physical encroachments there are the
10 psychic and soulish laws of life. And still above
these spiritual rules, cosmic equivalents.
While above all these, over everything are the
supreme moral commandments, the guiding rewards
that embrace the visible and the invisible.
Arts that are still unexpressed, the spiritual
arts, as yet unknown, tied to heavenly seasons,
unwrapped by wounded lips and inviolable
hearts from the unscrupulous future. For our dull
present where the possibilities are crippling
20 mankind and dreams ruin the lives, - the star-skirted
opportunities help not to be afraid of
the coming life. An exact knowledge that's rather
felt than conscious, which flows in the veins, about what's
happening beyond, makes us to live above life
while here, toward a goal. For we may stay upright,
truthful even amongst the criminally minded,
because these spiritual and moral rules have
no connections with the penal code of earth. We
guess, we suspect an existence above daily
30 survival in love, the feistivalish din of
cosmic landscapes where the vague indications
ensure that we are more healed than health calls for
and the heroism of love provides perspectives
even for cock-eyed observers. The right to be
born, the right to life, to decide about oneself....
We all are happy even if we don't feel it
as we may live according to a life beyond.

XXXVI

Improperia

We carry a piece of eternity with us
wherever we go and heaven is there where we're,
shining through the eyes and touching with gestures.
If one could draw the lines which connect the living,
the dead, with each other in a city above
family ties, we'd get a net from which not a
single heart would be left out. There is just one love
with many variant readings. For there cannot be
a spring outside without having it in the heart
10   also, - the oftenness compels one to rise
above moodspasms. A present enlarged to spatial
infinity where the dreams advance everything:
we are believers but not on religious ground.
To see the trees as medallions, decorations
on the landscape, honor-guards in standing firm though
they move with the wind and rain, - an elastic stance
goes along even with staunchness. Oh, happy are
those who do not notice the suffering, the pain
in their lives and overlook the sorrows, but pay
20   attention only to the joys, the lights, the arts...
Pray we should always be saved from those who are not
trying to learn from life, aren't improving themselves
and do not want to go ahead. That we may not
pilfer life on cheap pleasures, ashamed of lost times...
There are heroes who never complain or notice
difficulties, regardless of circumstances,
but glance ahead and help. Like every evening the
sun, we should depart by leaving a gorgeous dusk,
our unforgettable colorful twilight behind.

XXXVII

A Giant Secret

A giant secret is hidden in the universe
which is spread all over, into the whistling of
the birds, the reflected sunlight of the water,
into the languid breeze under the trees, and yes,
into the eyes. By mathematics perhaps, in
an equation, such as ten billion stars over
two eyes, the existence and whatness of the soul
could be expressed. Life has minutes, sometimes even
days when everything is questionable. Over
10   the works, goals of man, away from relatives, friends,
when the net of a faraway and very high
understanding is thrown, we wonder why the aim
of life is so low, such a pittance, and why the
essence of existence is so blurred? We would like
to believe that upon our departure the vast
meaninglessness of life, the inconsistencies
will be wiped out, will turn into the opposite...

Our spiritual world affects the material
cosmos in a strange way, - our concepts are confused
20   by the soulish plains and bodily conflicts, that
existence's contents sunk into biology
where constancy is eliminated... Poets
might devise explanations under metaphors:
lending ourselves to be misunderstood, we watch
as the berjerkers go on rampage and as the
idiocy spreads like the superwind in space...
Only the very hurt and the childish notice
that at evening time the sky is a spring field of
finches stretching from south to north and the dogwood
30   trees explode in the stillness like the sparklers or
ornaments, that children believe hang with the stars.

XXXVIII

Words are Jails

The words are jails, sometimes I felt, and into them
we lock ourselves, defining freedom over and
again. Used so often, words seem so recycled
that they have lost their charm and power by being
unable to indicate when and where the roads
of heaven curve down to earth. The lava lines of
poems scorching in the night, as well as touching
the hearts, but can't really point to and display the
many ways of seeing or the sizzling stillness
10 with the cosmic cooking of fate. The Men-o'-night
guysers and Truckist monks all agree on one thing,
namely that the concepts of the pilferati
cannot be squeezed into words, however much it's
Pressed by tear-ians or by Farmed a-suitical
all-egg-ations. Like Onionikos' *Knowed Book,*
or Julian of Forewhich's *Slangwich Book*, which was
plagiarized by both Stariyake Yimbo and
Mashitake Nu, as the viciously good and
bold Amenous of Itchigan demonstrated
20 it in the Gaylick language, - often it can happen
that a heart freezes over even in July...

XXXIX

We arrive

Being in immense peace with oneself and the world
is a condition of stepping higher inside.
The great humming of the universe which is used
nowadays to hang queer theories on, since the
instruments ceaselessly listen to it, is heard
within, it's the stream of elegant knowledge that
one receives, the faint echo of unuttered words.
Fasting minds and souls prepare for the vision where
the little flames one walks on, which burn without light,
10   are tamed, self-offering accompaniments to
the amethyst birds and the amber bees on the
flowering branches of our spring trees. We arrive.
Soundless rushing of an invisible river,
signals the time in that spiritual landscape.
It is not important what's the city outside,
it is not important what language's spoken there, -
the arrival is the focus, the end of the
pilgrimage. For wherever we are, there is home.

XL

The Sound-Trees

Sometimes we wish a lover wouldn't forget for our
sake what she owes to destiny, to her own goals
in life, to herself. And today, when it is so
fashionable to play beggars since the better
actors live longer, there are the invisible
consequences of change, as with the seasons that
pass over us. The tune- or sound-trees, dropping notes
like leaves are whirling down at autumn from the elms,-
a pinging sound is heard after another note, -
they're messages of limitless sincerity.
When they bloom melodies reach out of them, lulling.
And as the long-armed wind throws the discus of the
sun toward the west in the sky, I notice that
she throws her smile on everything around, even
on undeserving objects. My grumble beeing
stops with the darkness' fall when she stretches her arms
and I see the Big Dipper's ladle in her hand
doling out star-soup from the big bowl of the sky.

XLI

Revolutionized Seeing

The world is changing too fast. Very few people
stick to the old norms and values: the simple words
no longer suffice. It is an unfortunate
contradiction that we have to use the body
as a tool to open up higher regions for
observation, which, when it happens, is almost
always without the mind. But what is over
there, in that immaterial world, we can't guess,
it's only what the soul may see. In the rush of
10   life nowadays, there is less and less time for the
search. We may as well take up a collection for
the greedy, - or attend an international
concert for the deafinitely blind who unchant
their emotional savagery. For feelings are
instruments in life. Poetical luggages
illustrate that we are children of our time
rather than of our parents. Doing good isn't praised
anymore, only money, bad jokes with the sex.
Still on the slope of existence when one tries to
20   sound the glittering recalls of a region for
the truth-hungry, news-thirsty age, that with singing
as to become the song, - like long time ago when
religion was still a passion, - the effort is
to become the temple! Into the heights of
feelings we fly and with revolutionized
seeing we express the echoes from another
language, in stillness sometimes, when inspiration
and luck conspire with the rhythm and rhyme of the heart:
we do not live at all if we don't live inside.

PART TWO

A POETIC RECORD OF MY BEING

THE GUARDIAN OF HER DREAMS

We leave the dreams here. Even the best ones where you
saw that there were black crosses in the sun and moon.
Stars we see awakened in the smooth ebony
mirror of the sky as if we'd be sleeping while
walking, show us the reality with the truth
as the evening looks in through the many windows.
I cannot depart or escape while still you love,
until we are reborn in a different form
of life, another existence where one of the
10   rings of Saturn will be our wedding ring. It's hard to
keep the eyes dry and away the constant sorrows
from our existence. The *Idylls of the Queens* with
the Sea of Memory slide into the past where
our blooming apricot and mimosa trees are,
the owlets and the purple pirouettes of the
summer-end shadows, these strange mosaics of the
lawn in the aura of burning... Hummingbirds
hover in front of huge funnels of flowers so
motionless as I'm watching over the steady
20   stream of dreams. No wealth, regardless how great, and no
power will secure immortality, beckoned
by dreams, - only the cleanest enraptured spirit.
Goodness of the heart in itself is not enough.
To solve the greatest problems on earth one does need
only common sense and the determination
of a farmer. Prudency and sorrows in a
tied thought: as a woman stretches herself over
the naked body of a man, so intimately
with all their weight the dreams lie on us. Not from the
30   next world but from the third one, knowing more about
our future than anyone could ever suppose.
She has seen the rectangular souls with the great
network of organs inside, as if souls could be
pulled up from the earth without their knowledge with the
two long chords attached to them. She has seen three small

papersacks, two of them for mixing of life, one
for death, and she has seen angels without wings, - or
was I seeing them? - Walking on a rainbow she
stood on colored circular stairsteps, - watching those
40   who were one hundred times larger than we are, dressed
as corn-cob dolls. Light-dew on the stems under a
blue enameled sky, we are so weightless as the
figures of El Greco and will remain the same,
always like an apparition in the endless
almost ineffable silence of afterwards.
Exchanging dreams about kissing birds and horses,
as the tears are running down on the icicles:
drunken with the happiness of another kind,
we decorate immortality with the light-
50   kneaded sincerity of immobility.
Well-kept secrets, dreams recorded for ourselves, tied
with musical strings of the crickets to the hearts...

One may find great words beyond the deeds of others
but we find nothing behind the great words. Ajax
in the *Iliad*, we ask: "Raise up from the earth..."
For lovers are all prisoners of beauty like
real artists, never angry at those who are
departing, only the never arriving ones...
One's nobility is seated in the eyes, one's
60   goodness on the lips, his tolerance in the ears,
gentleness in his hands and in the thoughts greatess...

Aren't we all acrobats balancing ourselves
over dizzying dangers of death, while bragging
of superhuman achievements? To be wondered
at like shopwindow mannequins, we dance on a
rope, symbolizing a problem which we must solve.

Where feeling, knowledge and the silence stretch to light
and dreams with distances, pains into a subtle
guessing, a creative self-consuming fire burns
70   in every existing thing as invisible
giant, eddying places open behind them
and in the cool, sober awakening comes an
obvious other-thereness. Death pushes every
person into himself, into one's own pit as
objects no longer can hold or tie anyone
down: the cleanest and the most majestic may gain
their go ahead signs. Over black flames as something

very irritating and shocking looms with strange
appearance, even with beauty: those things which will
80 remain indeed deeply engraved, that were brought to
our attention by a blow: blond rivers braided
together in a dusk and chained to the sky by
blue butterfly wings, or the Pegasus Parade
in Louisville, where an inflated white horse is flown
above the head of spectators and where, like Job,
we also pretend to be fools, for the masses
we cannot prophesy what they would like to hear.

SILENCE SPEAKS WITH UNWORDS

On the timeless roads of a poet's words future
is addressed intimately, since the roads run up
to the skies and meet with the predictions. In the
open sky of the verse the good-deeds are the stars
and there, in the place of the sun, I'd paint the heart.
The words do not have their old meanings anymore,
they describe nothing and embrace not a being,
for they're impoverished, unembellished and few.
Indeed it is a separate language when one's
10   an intellectual. Odysseus returning
home docs not dare to tell anyone who he is:
the experiences of the past seventy
years make me feel humble. One must try not to live
according to the physics of this world.
Every poem is an attempt to overcome
the impossible, knowing not whether this fast
circling beyond-the-light universe is a new
wonder from the invisible world of atoms,
a dizziness, love or a little fever? The
20   remodelled Laocoons of the subways and the
pornograms of the tabloid press, the TV try
to convey we lost the control over ourselves.

The earth was in us much before it appeared on
the outside for the eyes. Ask any poet about
his wife and he'll tell you that the sky and earth are
her arms and the days are her dress to look always
fresh... Madness or a pride might prohibit us to
confess, the shadows of the trees are animals
walking as the flame-faced flowers are speaking with
30   the golden, flame-winged birds. Creation is an utmost
concentration, for over every temptation
the poet is the master, carrying his lines
from before birth as we all carry small, blooming
gardens within... Stars, shoveled into mountains, while
tiny crescent moons hang on the trees around, like
gravity waves, the speeding fall of objects, a
word, a sigh, a side-glance or a long, intended

silence: a voice from beyond, above the living,
as a law, a limit, order or message, a
40 voice calls inside, urges, demands to work on our
human future. Looking at the bombed ruins of life,
the poverty, left to us as an heirloom with
hunger, - we overwhelmed ourselves. To fare the same
fate on earth, as Dante sought, - glancing with his stern
eyes, - the good are persecuted and there are too
many who are good only out of sheer revenge.

There are two springs on the Isle of the Blest, - said
Pomponius Mela, - one causes instant death
by laughter and the other to be born again.
50 As if eyes could create the wonders, the world is
presented anew. Written but not by words, in
the space of the inner eyes where seeing cannot
cover the end, years are woven into large
tapestries of centuries, the embering fruits,
the unspoken suggestions of flowers and the
waving walls of violet-wrought visions where the light
oozes with the breeze, sparks of a newly breaking
dawn, - the world sings as one person. Seasons run
in a reverse manner, writing circles outside
60 of the globe, of an eternal surrealism.
And the poet, madly in love, collects for a
song the harmonies of heaven, the pains, the dreams
with which the unmusical wind spreads and splashes
the saintly, almost unthinkable heroic stance
of his spouse, the love that radiates throughout life,
that pure fire, the light, the summer heat, the heart.

PART THREE

The following four cantos, completed while the second and third volumes of my NOVA COMOEDIA were in the printer's hands, intended to be inserted there, namely into Pt. II, after Canto 91, p. 108, as well as into the Contents note on p. 7. The first three cantos here, GULLIVER AMONG THE WINGED HORSES, PT. III (new Canto 92), THE EGGHEADS (Canto 93) and THE RUM AGE (Canto 94) are parts of MODERN SATIRES, namely F), G) and H). THE INNOCENTING PROCESS (Canto 95) refers to the Innocentizing (The Second Eating of the Apple or Absolution from Sin).The total lines in the three parts of the work with these additions are now 16,232 in 150 cantos.

GULLIVER AMONG THE WINGED HORSES

III

92

Since Plato said somewhere that unbelief in God
is a disease, and that injustice is also
an illness when it is maintained within, health of
the body became an aesthetic symptom, a
210 symbol of the views held by one. But nowadays
all the good things are locked in a Pin-door-a box,
and only the bad things are out, parading at
large in the world, many are flushtrated and few
are the chewsers. Out of the ought-to-nary life
hurrysome people, believing in and often
depending on palliticians, usually are
victims of foolanthropy, - they accept grants that
tie them with exaggerated understanding
to predictable dreams. Of course there is nothing
220 wrong with having some dreams that are predictable,
that is short term dreams, loans, which one gets by pawning
long-term interests. The frighternity of the winged
horses fed on gripefruits, stolen illusions and
crudimentary grudge-matches, has already
"truthified" their present, as the "Cold Minor's Daughter"
did express it once in Utless, Pitchigan. She
said, - or was it Annie Mosity, outfluenced
by the bearoccracy, who said it ? - that one hates
to be bitter in retrospect, but nothing in
230 the world plays to the hands of those who're waiting at
home for a miracle to happen, that they will
hit the jackpot. This sounds as an accidental
curse or perhaps even a blessed curse, but those who
brood on thoughts accumulate an unpayable
debt of gratitude in directing them and thus
solving some problems. May heaven hear them, as once
Desdemona was told, whose real name, by the way,
was Does Demon. Ah, she had detourminations
and chest not, so being far from smurfection, as her
240 distant cousin Leonard Convincy was, she, too,

became the member of the arrestedcracy
when walking along the nightstreets although she wasn't
in need of money. Going back to the horses
with wings, the colorful Rhymebow celebrations
never burden the participants, listeners
with uncontrolled display of emotions or violent
expressions of feelings, however powerful these
may be. That the Rhymebow celebrations are not
identical with the Annual Poetry Day
250 Recitals and with the National Holiday
festivities does not need to be said at all,
because rhymebows are pulled like little flags on poles,
similar to the Tanabata Festivals
in Japan. On the bow-size flags are sayings
painted, naturally in rhyming couplets, and
waved high above the heads, shaken above the manes.

It was the axiom of Boris Goodenough,
who was unable to give a single good reason
to live, that the terrortories of his empire
260 extend from Smellgoland, which he called Hellgoland,
to the Turnip-pikes of the Winged Horses. He had
a herring aide and if he wrote anything, he
wrote a dendron, because his favorite flowers was
a rhododendron. The best of the winged horses,
among them Spickory Hick from Pillage, Stirtius
McBribe and S.K. Fritz O'Phrinic reached at a
Putty Day Parade, agreed that every line of
a poem is a black hole that pulls one's heart in
its direction unawares. There was also a
270 spooffocating agreement on the seductive
effect of the maranga rhythm on the island
of Puerto Rico. However, this is not sure
and so might be taken with a whole train of salt. In
the sales-storms, stirred up by the beggarnauts and the
enhancers of opportunities, oblivious
to niceing, the earsoreous conversations
usually result in a spin-itch, which is not
identical with the green spinach, sold in the stores.

Ignorance is the greatest disease of the soul,
according to Plato, so the overeager
pursuance of matters related to poetry
contests, study or investigation of an
280 unidentified flying metaphor, or a

flowing pattern is strictly not in the public
interest, since many times these are carried on
with controversy and contention which shakes the
soul and tears it to pieces. So the word-battles,
even in scintillaferous disguise or in
a dawndelionized fashion only detract from
the pleasure of playing schizophrenic games, from
the psychopathic intermittency. The winged
horses, nevertheless, are totally convinced
290 that when the end of time comes, at the very end
of everything, of the world, there will be the Word.

In the privacy of their homes they all suffer
their own hell, as Alonedrias expressed it once.
He was the author of *Three Mouths-Cat-Ears*, to which
a commentary was written by Samuel
Furtatowich, the Unblessed bachelor. He was
from Pitlah, Rushia. Alonedrias also proved
that it was not the Pin-door-a-box where all the
good things were locked but a Pundora box.
300 This was an exsceptionally great disclosure
which, nevertheless, was pinned on the doors of the
guyscrapers in Tall-a-hussie, and was left as
a hareloom for mankind. Esther Roach,- the friend of
Monsieur Gaga from Rochester, - who always drank
poorvoisier since her sight was failing, though
she ate heartichoke with grievey sauce which is said
to prevent blindness, so Esther Roach in a column,
published by inkrements, reported that the raw
heartichokes, that is the cores of artichokes, are
310 dullicious, specially after jam-and-tonic.
·Since she was always concerned with food and cooking,
she wore a parsley necklace and a pumpkin-skirt
and she also gave the title to her column:
"Ultomato". She was Ogden nashish in her
writing, uncriticizeable, and bitten by
a luna tick, eventually ended up in
a painitentiary, still writing her column which,
set in stanzas like poems, was saturated
with goriness and uninterrupted mayhem.

G) THE EGGHEADS

One would think that the eggheads live in a special
country where the airlines require visas with the
tickets. This assumption is wrong, for the eggheads
are to be found everywhere on earth. Naturally,
there are people whose heads look like a cube, square,
and others with heads circular or globular,
resembling the planets. Pretensions go a long
way, so the eggheads received their distinctions not
from the peculiar intellectual interests
10   they were pursuing but from the formation of
the skull, from the elongated egg-shaped hairless
contours which is just as difficult to deny
as to accept it. At no time were the eggheads
called hairyticks, since they never possessed bushy
hair-dos. Determinatus, who was born either
in Ravington or in Shallweville, and was twice
as blind as one who lost his eyesight when young, used
to say in his Frenchish accent that "much people
and many money cannot make one, anyone
20   egg-a-liter-ian". But that was said before
the groan-embargo was instituted and the
irradiated food would have affected his
hammerhoids. Figuratively speaking, the
zero-minded and unstrengthtative predictions
about a horrendarium never can be
substantiated since the unobservations
do not add up. And creating small black holes for
commercial purpose and turning some optical
components into kinetic ones are, at the
30   present time, beyond the ability of science.
The head of the Eggheads is Heggeda, also
called El Chapitano, who imagines himself
to be a bamboostador from Thawed-Shick-Istan
or Jinnytoba. In insumulatious moods
he could be quite charming with members of any
dailygations, especially when he is
not in his cylindered or unexpanded state.

When the eggheathers are blooming, as soon as the
blasted ball games are over, a festival is
40   organized. The march of the heads alone, complete
in themselves, precedes the celebrations. The heads
actually are rolling in the best sense of
the word, since they are not burdened with bodies and
arms. The impression is given that a kind of
imagenetic force moves them. Separated from
the body, hands removed, the thinking globular
heads produce the purest possible vision since
they are not contaminated with earthly chores.

Heggeda's Prime Minister is Miss Chief, who used
50   to slough it off when confronted with saintsational
aleggations. She ridiculed the charges in
a mayish, perhapsian manner, as if those
would have been just sarkisstic and hintalating
personal attacks, without any substance. But
meggalomania is a serious problem
for the eggheads. Even a minuschool amount
of it can ruin one's reputation. The more so
since the majority of the population
is egg-is-compellian, and for them even
60   a tiny self-eggrandizment is dangerous.
Miss Chief, for instance, when she was queening around,
never took a collect call from her own stomach,
meaning the "très jolie" défartment, since, said she,
"no one can défart before the occurrence of
serious things". That is before knowing when fartune
will appear. Which leads to the most important point,
namely that if we are here, where is there at all?
For life is a disposable commodity...

Unfocussing the attention, we should discount
70   the notion that because of resemblance Miss Chief
could be called as our Money Lisa. For it takes
so much gall to assert this that one can win the
Gallic Wars, even the garlic wars, with such an
impudence. By spring each year the marchuary
papers wrote, till writeousness caught up with them, that
the too well-known figure of the Money Lisa,
Miss Chief, was an eggscuse only. By then they were
threatened with eggscommunication or worried
that they'll be eggsorcised by someone from the Far
80   Write, who uses his pen as a pendulum to

hurt, slabberghast His Eggscellency Heggeda
and his eggileptic son, Ohnosiderus
in the city Eggsilanty, where they pronounce
egg'onomics with a broken eggcent and the
freggrance is used very infregguently because
long time eggo they all went to wrongturnity.

The impolite ears heard whatever they were not
supposed to hear and as Mrs. Highdy Lowha
so vigoratively eggspressed in the monthly
90   Noticery, the eyes degreated what they saw.
She was a real zinger together with her
sister Burnadebt, who married Impolitus
in his eightiest year and became the best known
fartcasters on yolklore without a quenchion mark.
But Mrs. Lowha was not in her worstness when
she said that the mouths "were peelandering on
unhopeable fruits", because appetitis,
making a circuistic design on the faces
as they were lawndering along the boulevards when
100 the sun was running like a horse, did not unhalt
the parade padded with intensibility.
The inquasareal motion of the march was
maintained by a cancering wiggle, invented
by a Wyatt Herb, which empowered the heads to
assume cosmic rotations in deflative terms,
with some unformed objects from the vanishing point
under the symbol of a crucified red rose
of the web-designed, fresh, clean, verse-embroidered sky.

H) THE RUM AGE

There was a time in mankind's history which was
characterized by constant drinking, dope and crime.
The alcohol most favored during this time was
rum, so social historians like to refer
to this period as the rum age. But rum age
is more infamous for what wasn't said about it
publicly, namely the dark side of life,
the scurrilities, the surquedry and the self-
conceit it involved. And the darker side was more
10 dark than it can be described since almost without
exception everybody was affected. The
hieroglyphic great stairway at Copan in
Honduras does not portray more beasts from Mayan
time than life reveals today. Because the young are
so brazen, so audacious nowadays, they give
the impression of turnmites that turn the stomachs.
The fiendish display of sex, the spasmodistic
and tantrumscopic moves about it leave no room
for anything else. Kakecookieko Slynam
20 and the groggynoggian Marge Blabington
were the representatives of a movement
which spread from the Mud-a-Terrainian Sea and
the Dare-Daknells to the fartification of
Cheapheton by the vowcano. Intestions displayed,
and nothing held back, since there was no such thing as
private parts, - the youth, dressed in manure, swam in it.
Illiterally speaking, both of these persons
flagellantly and quite larcenously attacked
everybody, as if they would have been deeprived
30 of the senses or would have had no drain itch. The
damage caused on the nower generation can't
be estimated. The state suffered most. Culprit
America was the target of the lowest
esteem, which to them meant the corporate callprits.
As one who loses his competence on a cue,
the people started to drink rum instead of the
usual water. Even bread and cakes were dipped
in rum, meat was sprinkled with it and it was offered
as baptismal holy water and communion

40   drink. Rumming through the ages as someone would be
      looking for something, only imprecations were
      unearthed, recriminatory homilies, all
      tainted with rum. The indelicacy of the
      situation was complicated by the fact
      that the politicians, under the influence,
      began to speak in acronyms like many of
      the anchor persons. Since no one could understand
      them, they became respectable and politeticks
      became the trade-mark of their profession.

50   At the Summer Salting Festivals in Woodlouse
      where the ruddimental prepowderance of things
      required not to eat sanewiches, the vainial
      absorbation produced a joinalism. This was
      mustard-minded either by Pushimus or by
      Pope Ular's galactrified posttance, namely that
      lies never can be exhausted since there are so
      many of them. The bulldozerites, already
      the victims of success, jumped on the bandwagon
      and distributed frettacini cakes to the
60   Coney Island-minded, cascading in thick mire.

      Not Soak-Rates, Plait-Toe, nor the members of
      Ratary Clubs in their warbecuing outings
      could predict where rum age might take us.
      As an offterthought, it was offered either by
      Concommitatus or Riftolaus in one of
      their indiscreetly published writings, that we live
      in a cultural Bronze Age, perhaps even in
      Hell Addict times. The ghastliary invention
      of songora, the key-bored combination of
70   song and organ, certainly proved there was so much
      inertgy left unspent that heorsheizing
      maneuvers, private rites of deification were
      all doomed with plumetology and jingoism.

      Because earritations became so common, some
      calmpetitions were instituted where silence-
      rehearsals replaced the thermostatic binges
      and the uprearious fakeulty meetings. It was
      in Elle-annoy where a don'toydarty peace was
      hammered out, giving a temporary relief.
80   However, the peace was not universally
      accepted because it was signed on Spite Day, and

in many ways it was a Daedalizing farce.
A very strange word, olykorabilis was the
key used by the applaudisti in the service
of foreign powers. For the art is different
now, a Moz art: Lewd, Whig, Fun, Bee, Though, When, all the
fuzzicians play the unguency, nicentennial
nooklear pieces. The particulture's ended. And
The Waste Land was replaced by The Waist Band even
90   on Why Kicky Beach, where rumba is the hit-dance.

The ex-scentric bruhaha of the lives contrasts
with the moods. Low and beehold: ricetiousness springs from
the lips of those freaks who parade in pleated skirts
pleading and in baggy pants begging, refinding
the barsenal of potato-chipsies... Well, one
can't use words from a dictionary to describe
the citizens of Upalongcia, who rap
to the tune of "Let the good times roll in, let the
good times roll...", unmindful of the carking load that
100 burdens the spirit since they have no such thing in
them. How would the careless know that misery doesn't
let them look up and see that past the sin-extracts
which are sky-high, there are the Carpetian Hills,
the azure carpets of Heaven, the galorified
slopes, the peaks of permanence..! On earth, it seems, we
are viewing a Rear-End Theatre, with gallows and
horrorscopes, while forgetting that we have inside
and outside eyes, arms of the soul, of unequal
length which may reach and touch God's tunic or his socks.

110 It must be noted that the countries mentioned live
in mockracy, except those stated otherwise.
Runagate pretentionaires, Socrathief, Rachel
Slurs, Venedetta Brr, the toughly Ticia Jus,
Burrtholomew Healthyforas of Istvahan,
tried to inflict punytive damages on the
states by declaring the Sortofarians be
ex-platonists, crystal-bowl-gazers, who're
looking for reign-checks. They were singing a strange song,
"Hit no pot, oh moose!" to the accompaniment
120 of a womandolin, when they were struck by some
rightonitis, seemilarly to pesternauts
in trying to create grand puddly images...
They 'd art disease, all, and died of heroic silence.

In the year of the Ramification King Joe
was installed by playing the picklelows and the
drumsticks. As he was small, he was addressed as "Your
Royal Smallness", like Alexander the Small was.
All the painters of Barbarizon were good in
illustrating the high event in front of some
130 bringerbread houses where schitzy bragpipe bruises
were eliminated from eyeshots, and large green
worry-berries were sprinkled on top of human
rights puddings. The liesy Count Orgazm insisted
on naming the day Wind'sday, because the wind was
so great that it bent the chimneys of factories
as a modern hero bowling with muscaline
would do it at moon soon time. The effect was clear
classical trickonometric, assumotive
illgebra. One did remark "the trunkillity
140 kills us. Even the angels inhale their halos..."
which was indeed correct to describe the happenings.
The most unpleasable was the nose thrill of the
noise, which sent many people packing. But King Joe
was not joking, - he meant business. And he ordered
taverknackles and spoofermarkets be closed and
detourgents distributed free to smelletrons,
which was an absolutely doomitable gesture,
affecting even the snowbodies in making
havoc with the normal funktioning of society.
150 The greatest embarfment occurred when pesternauts
were ordered to scale the Eyefull-tower in town
to clean. But that's the story for another time.

THE INNOCENTING PROCESS

After the Rum Age came a sober era
in which the excesses of the past were trimmed
or totally eliminated. As if
Botticelli's beautiful Primavera
would have come alive now with a whirlwind

of activities, changes that were massive,
and art, sense as well as proportion restored
to a glory which they seldom had before.
Beauty, the inner one, became impressive
10   and important enough for some to afford.

The wars and crime were the catharsis that tore
out the unwanted and the shameful from us
and human nature was somehow magnified
and lighted. With a secret universe's door
opened, the rum only led to a rumpus

room within, where many wrong emotions died
and many juvenal starts were sung to death.
In the Museum of Heaven the defeated
time-pieces and periods were side by side,
20   certain centuries where a jump in progress

lifted mankind higher, now exhibited,
with rhymeless suspension of sounds the ensphered
vision of the soul stood along the wrecked times.
Catharsis refers to the age which fêted
sin, sex and stomachs, that always interferred

with the fast ongoing pagan pantomimes
and constituted the riddance from the sins,
liberation from chains which were on the minds.
Sins, acquired by our forebears in Paradise,
30   ceased to exist. Like from sealed bottles the jinns,

they boiled out of existence with many kinds
of inherited beliefs. Deliverance
from the old concepts of living nigh entailed
giving up the confession booths and the finds
of psychiatrists for an inner advance.

That beauty disguises pain and can't be failed
to show a vast system of dreams was obvious
by our return to pre-Edenic days.
Not the treasury of the Topkapi, the veiled
40   vaults of the Vatican or the fabulous

riches of the Schatzkammer, the golden trays
of kings and queens, nor the exquisitely wrought
jewels of the past can match the simple joy
of smiles, surpassing pleasures with which one pays
his respect, crowning words of a sincere thought.

For beauty is a mark like on a lake a buoy,
as much inside as it is outside to watch.
One is being made innocent by the newly
consumed applely symbolism and by the coy
50   desire to tread the road of the apple patch...

The Righter, The Honester see the ruly
drive, see the time ahead, ages that will come
with a bounty that'll from now only increase,
and not tax the expectations unduly,
but will represent a permanent income.

Through Telepathic Poems the poet sees
that one no longer can inherit the sins
or punished for unhappened allegations.
I proclaim deliverance from a disease
60   as from some unnecessary disciplines.

Looking through untold tragedies, delusions,
the bard sees through the pretentions of the rich
and hides his tears in the sleeves, - an old habit. -
But he does not believe that with the fusions
ethics and religion could create a bridge.

The doctrine of evil is no more valid,
no longer acceptable. It is a claim,
a philosophic one, perhaps a legal,

but from human nature it should be so split
70   as from wrong the good deeds, holy and profane.

Celesticated, disrobing the meagre
expectations, we do not stretch the desires,
nor exchange the dreams, just objectively state
what Nietzsche and many others were eager
to condemn, and burn on the flames of fires.

For it was long and quite useless a debate
to get rid of our traditions and the past
or change some of them, change them for the better.
Like in a court of law it's endless the wait
80   and to change the statutes never will be fast.

It is good to be good. But as a quester
of eternal values, one can't emphasize
immateriality, the soul enough,
that's stripped of the encroachments of the letter
and spirit of punishment or sacrifice.

Vice is a human concept. It was a rough
device and deterrent, which superimposed
on incurable souls gained some acceptance
and spread to other fields, earning only scoff.
90   But it wasn't a genetically endorsed

concept and in its effect, insouciance,
it contradicted nature and destiny.
Time does not honor anyone. And it seems
it's against human endeavour, the expanse
of knowledge, of life, even morality.

We ought to step outside of it. With the breeze
the bare branches of winter trees will bring
back attention to the empty labyrinths
that encharm the spirit which summertime sees,
100 hears the scarlet and azure macaws prattling.

ANNOTATION ON THE MARGIN

(Canto 80, Smell-Lands VIII, addition to p 71,
after 25 unnumbered lines)

It's the duty of posterity to set the records
straight and provide also alternative views regarding
the departing of Hellyodorous. A medical
panel, consisting of Siliager of Hyenasport,
30   Cinna Monna of Gasexstan, Sickostratus, either
of Maniacpolis or Malaiseia, who was a
retired badmiral, confined to the Dependagone,
as well as Welcome X, who came out of fretirement just
for the occasion, - well, this medical panel came to the
conclusion in a riflery, newsansical manner,
that Hellyodorous' porch-chops should not have been sniffed or
smelled at all, because their smell carried tricky noses.
I forbear to comment on their views expressed beyond
the fact that the team had an amazing capacity
40   for irrelevancy, by making extremely inneffective
guesses and sacrificing scientific approaches
wrapped in dreams, half-truths and a gaffe...Detestis...

At the time of the Bortion Battle of Buffalo, with the
conclusionary tactics of Briand the Unblessed,
Feteolatus, the Chief Stencher from Failadelphia,
a souperjerk wallowing in self-pity, on the urge
of Helpisedekh from the Hotel Healton,
on the analogy that the word kingdom, royaume is masculine
while la républic is feminine in French, brazenly
50   suggested that the biograspy or lifestory of
a woman should be called herstory and not history.

There was more to meet the required taste in this suggestion
as Gene the Awful, a follower of Rabelaistroix
remarked about Feteolatus, Hellyodorous
and the rest, by saying that "...they have all the wealth of the
world and I have an opinion of them", although he
never said what his opinion was. He did wield the
English language as no one else could, his best poetry
lines were those which he didn't write down. Bruce Unfit, who

60   was the mugisterial inkcarnation of Oakre-Teas in arrowganting,
stressed in a book, entitled *The Battle of Hatings*, that
certain life-stories were biteographies, made from shrillac
for telaversions, pokeloristic, lawndered bunji-tales,
and cannot be considered countrybutions to literarey
life even by pooritans, funamentalists or
praisidents of clubs, such as dummy-tummy Undo is,
heading the fakeful group of pawsitively Rehabed & Repoed.

Real goreyfication cannot rest on the interventional
cease-the-matic thesis that because one is too proud
70   to die, should be accorded special status among the
living. The literary bankrupts and the sicker minds,
or even the sickier conscienceless people, such
as Sotericus or Jaroslaw Passanovich were,
those who survived of pesterized milk, wishy-water and
lullypops, also called the shallow-wieners or
interwieners because they were catering to the plebs
with heartbreakery and intimidatis in their works,
called glowmances, were all yourselfish individuals.

Sir Jean d'Harms, the purposeario, or Betweena Killmekoff
80   should not even be mentioned. The first was Oedipified in
his kettle-ac in Singagapoor, the second died of omenitis
in a Matisserie off the Archipelag Gulash.
But because nowadays it is juicefied to wear the
underwear over sweaters, jackets and blouses in
certain circles and, as in a myth, the most awful
people live in the TV in a thoughless, totally
whoreticulturalist manner as snow-ghosts or steam-dummies,
the muzzled eyes should be covered by eye-muffs, otherwise
these insected people will not remain me-nor-i-ty,
90   but step out of their itzibishi Simpletoniads.

These gunks were always at the end of the human spectra
and properly regarded as endyviduals.
Because they advertise themselves with slogans: "The best deal
ever!" "No sooner the better!" "Same as cash!", over
the music of gutterdammerung of Wagner, while
hoping for some takers, a few more yous and mes, to buy
their product. The trend is universal, from Goodapest
to Sorrycuse or Toast-a Rica, where Toscaninny
used to live, before the holidays were smeared with the song:
100 "It is the time to be jealous, tralalala-la, la-la, la, la..."

PART FOUR

TELEPATHIC SONGS

I

I was traveling in a light, folding chair,
  propelled by a wheel behind, - in the air.
It was a personal helicopter,
  like a bicycle but a little lighter.

  Under me the California coast
was unfolding like a map or a picture.
  I didn't feel any sensation. The most
I felt was a pleasant ride on a fixture,

  a natural feeling. Although alone
on my helicopter, no one seemed to care
that someone, I, was flying above on
  my very simple machine in the air.

II

Even if someone wants to be very strict
with himself in looking ahead into the endlessness of time,
    'tis not too difficult to see and predict
that you will still love me when we both will no longer be alive.

Pearl from a little sand in the oyster shell
under the gentle rocking year-thousands in a symbolic dance:
    a tear in the soul of a poet will swell,
will grow into a vision of unearthly scope and brilliance.

III

It is impossible that we'd awaken each morning
from the dreams about one with whom we're in love.
With closed or open eyes what we do is hoarding
as if to see and feel would not be enough.

It's so strange to make it to summer and fall,
and observe daytime and again a night
when from a copper colored tree as a scandal
the wind chases the milk-scented fog in sight.

It is impossible that we are born only to die
and being in love we would not be like others,
unable to tolerate injustices. Why
would we try to second guess God or someone else?

I see only wondrous times to come, only autumns
with cold celebrations where the afternoon fire glints
in the fireplace and through the flames' hardly heard hums
one knows God visits him more often than he thinks.

IV

Perhaps I was playing but with utmost honesty
in converting the songs of birds into thoughts and words
to forget the dark history of man, the filthy
events through the awful generations of the earth.

For those who live today life is the biggest caper,
though the weights are more than any scale would ever show.
In the fields mothers work back-breaking. In a theater,
the sons play themselves up to an oligarchish glow.

And speak of their country, heckling, as a company,
where everybody steals, like a flim-flam man who flips.
But heaven nevertheless sets it afire in a great hurry
just to fulfill the well-prophesied apocalypse.

The offended mountains look, as the roofs, the streets:
will death occur now? Do we still have hearts? Or mercy?
Or do we know the proletariat in defeats
learns how immeasurable is the power of decency?